Contents

About phonics

Phonics is a method of teaching reading used extensively in today's schools. At its heart is an emphasis on identifying the *sounds* of letters, or combinations of letters, that are then put together to make words. These sounds are known as phonemes.

Starting to read

Learning to read is an important milestone for any child. The process can begin well before children start to learn letters and put them together to read words. The sooner children can discover books and enjoy stories and language, the better they will be prepared for reading themselves, first with the help of an adult and then independently.

You can find out more about phonics on the Usborne Very First Reading website, **www.usborne.com/veryfirstreading** (US readers go to **www.veryfirstreading.com**). Click on the **Parents** tab at the top of the page, then scroll down and click on **About synthetic phonics**.

Phonemic awareness

An important early stage in pre-reading and early reading is developing phonemic awareness: that is, listening out for the sounds within words. Rhymes, rhyming stories and alliteration are excellent ways of encouraging phonemic awareness.

In the following stories, your child will soon identify common sounds, such as the *a* as in **giraffe**; the *i* as in **chimp**; the long *i (i-e)* as in **sp<u>i</u>d<u>e</u>r**; the *ee* as in **hyena**; the *ea* as in **seal** and the long *a (a-e)* as in **<u>a</u>p<u>e</u>**. Each story has lots of fun rhymes to look out for, and there are puzzles at the end of the book for further practice.

Hearing your child read

If your child is reading to you, don't rush to correct mistakes, but be ready to prompt or guide if he or she is struggling. Above all, give plenty of praise and encouragement.

Giraffe in the bath

Giraffe's in her garden.

She tugs up thick weeds...

then digs a
big border

and plants
leafy trees.

9

Giraffe is tired out.

She trots up the path.

"Now I'm grubby and muddy.
I need a hot bath."

She jumps in the tub,
with a splish and a splosh.

The bubbles float upwards.
She gets set to wash...

The phone goes...

RING RING!

She runs to reply.

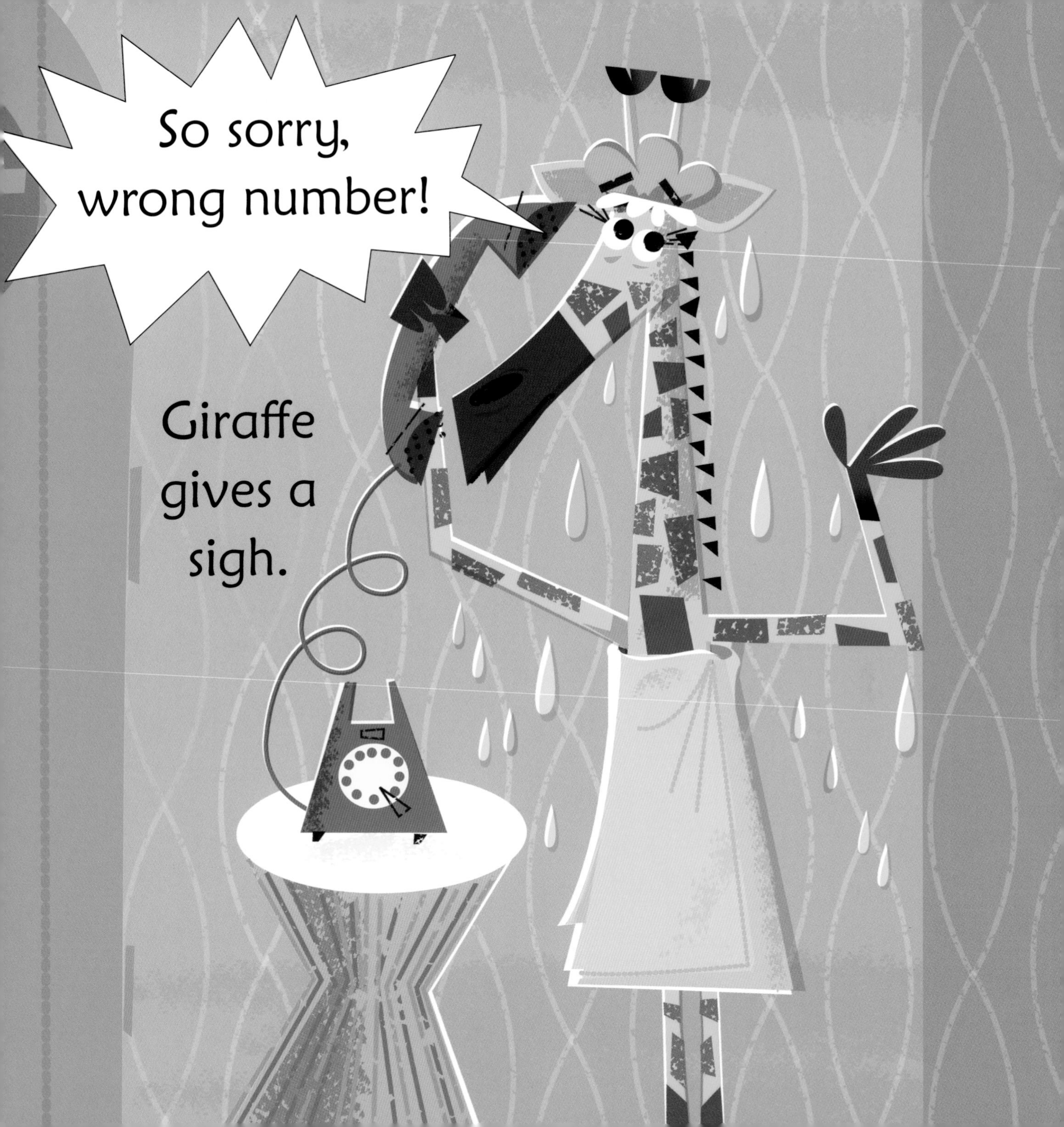

Giraffe gives a sigh.

Then three minutes later...
'Knock, knock!'
at the door.

A package for Jackal.

Not me, that's for sure!

Giraffe tries to relax,
with her eyes tightly shut.

But Baboon backs his truck...

Whoops!

...through the side of her hut!

The bath tub goes sliding,
through slippery soap.

It glides out of the door,
down a really steep slope.

"Look out!" shouts Giraffe,
her voice all a-quiver.

Ten zebras take cover,
as she heads to the river.

With a crash and a splash,
Giraffe lands by a raft.

Soon her bathtub is bobbing
past lots of odd craft.

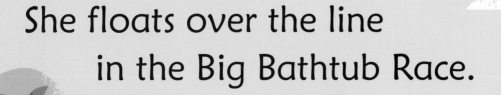

She floats over the line
in the Big Bathtub Race.

"What a win!" cries the judge.
"Here's your prize for first place!"

Chimp with a limp

"Hurray!" sings Chimp.
"I'm off to play.

I'll swing and slide and ride all day."

He nears the gate.
Then he hears, "Wait!"

It's Cheetah
with a heavy crate.

"Can you help me haul this home?
It's hard to heave it on my own."

But cheeky Chimp
pretends to limp.

I'm sorry. I'm a
limping chimp.

You're limping! Chimp, what did you do?

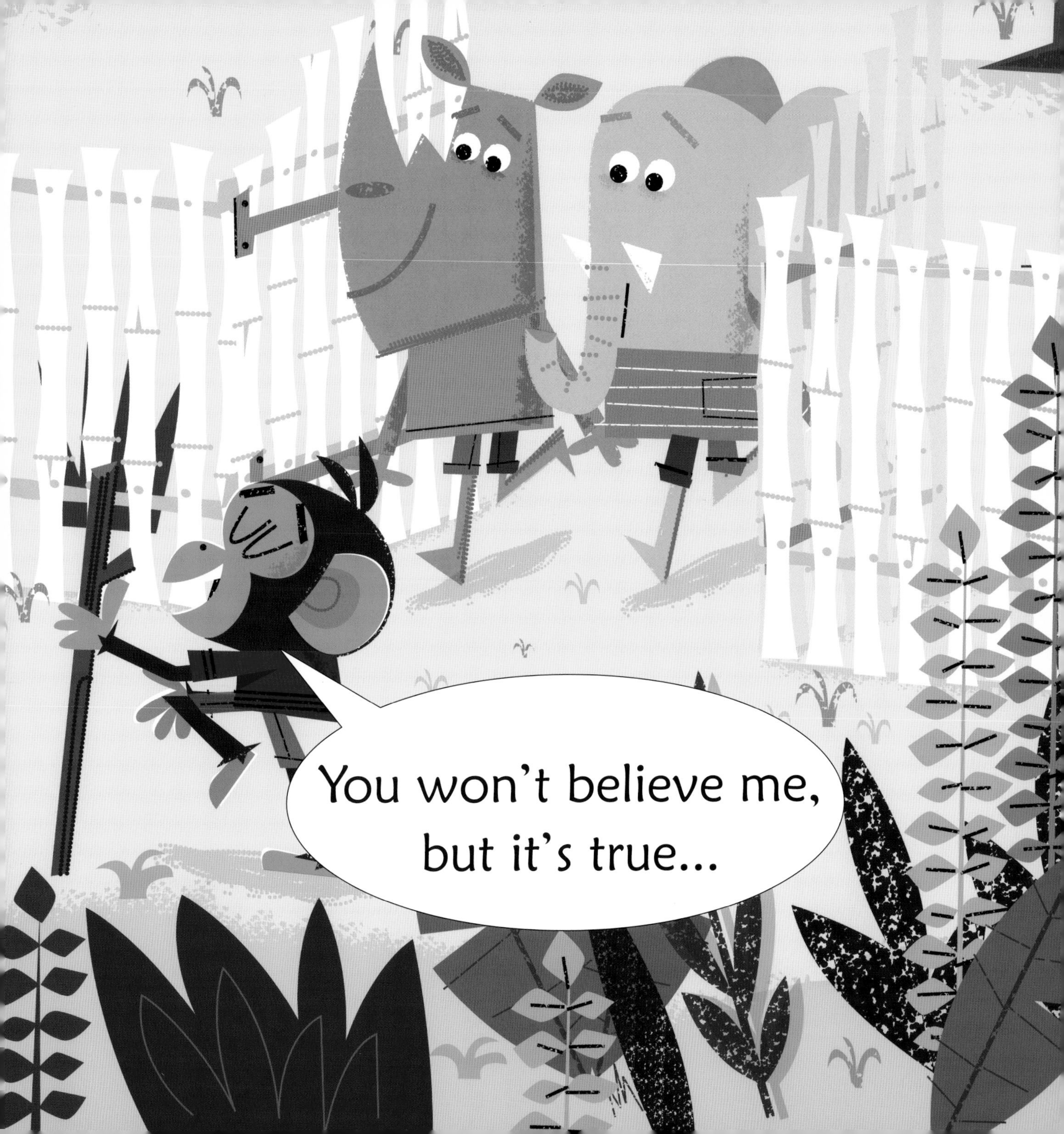
You won't believe me, but it's true...

I caught some pirates stealing gold...

...I fought them. I was feeling bold.

I tripped and slipped
upon the deck.

One slung a hook
around my neck.

They made me walk the plank you see...

...and, well, I fell into the sea.

I almost drowned.

Then it went dark.

I found I was inside a shark!

"Ha! Ha! Great joke," croaks Frog.
"Some tale."

"It WAS a shark," says Chimp,
"or whale."

It gave a burp.
I shot out...

SMACK!

...and landed in a black yak pack.

I had a hunch I'd be their lunch.

*They looked a hungry,
munching bunch.*

I ran until I reached my door,

battered, bruised
and oh, so sore.

Frog frowns. "I'm sure you **are** okay.
I saw you on your way to play."

"You have no limp, Chimp?"
Cheetah growls.

Am I a chump?

Now Cheetah scowls.

"You cheating Chimp!"
The chase is on.

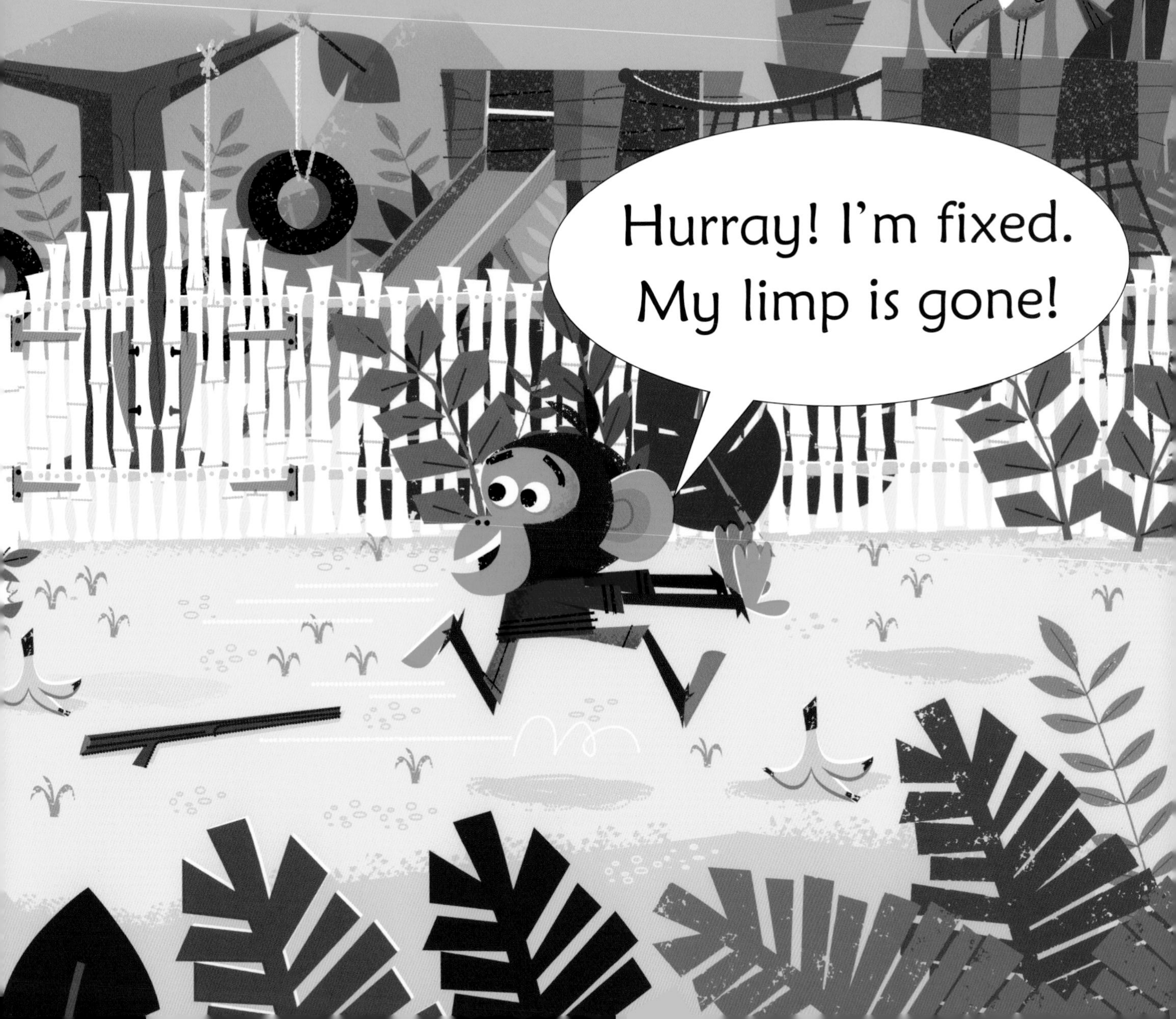

Spider in a glider

Spider is spinning her sparkling strings.

Swaying from branches,
she sings as she swings.

"I wish to fly

so I'm making some wings!"

She creeps
up a rock

and then leaps
into space.

What a shock! With a splat,
she lands flat on her face.

"I'll try it again.
I will fly!" declares Spider.

She falls even harder,
but Beetle has spied her.

"I can't fly either,"
sighs Beetle, beside her,
"though I tried and I tried.

So... I built my own glider!"

The glider is gleaming
and ready to ride.

Beetle and Spider
both clamber inside.

Dragonfly tows them up...

...high in the sky.

Then Beetle
lets go...

They glide in
wide circles

and ride on
the breeze.

The wind blows below them...

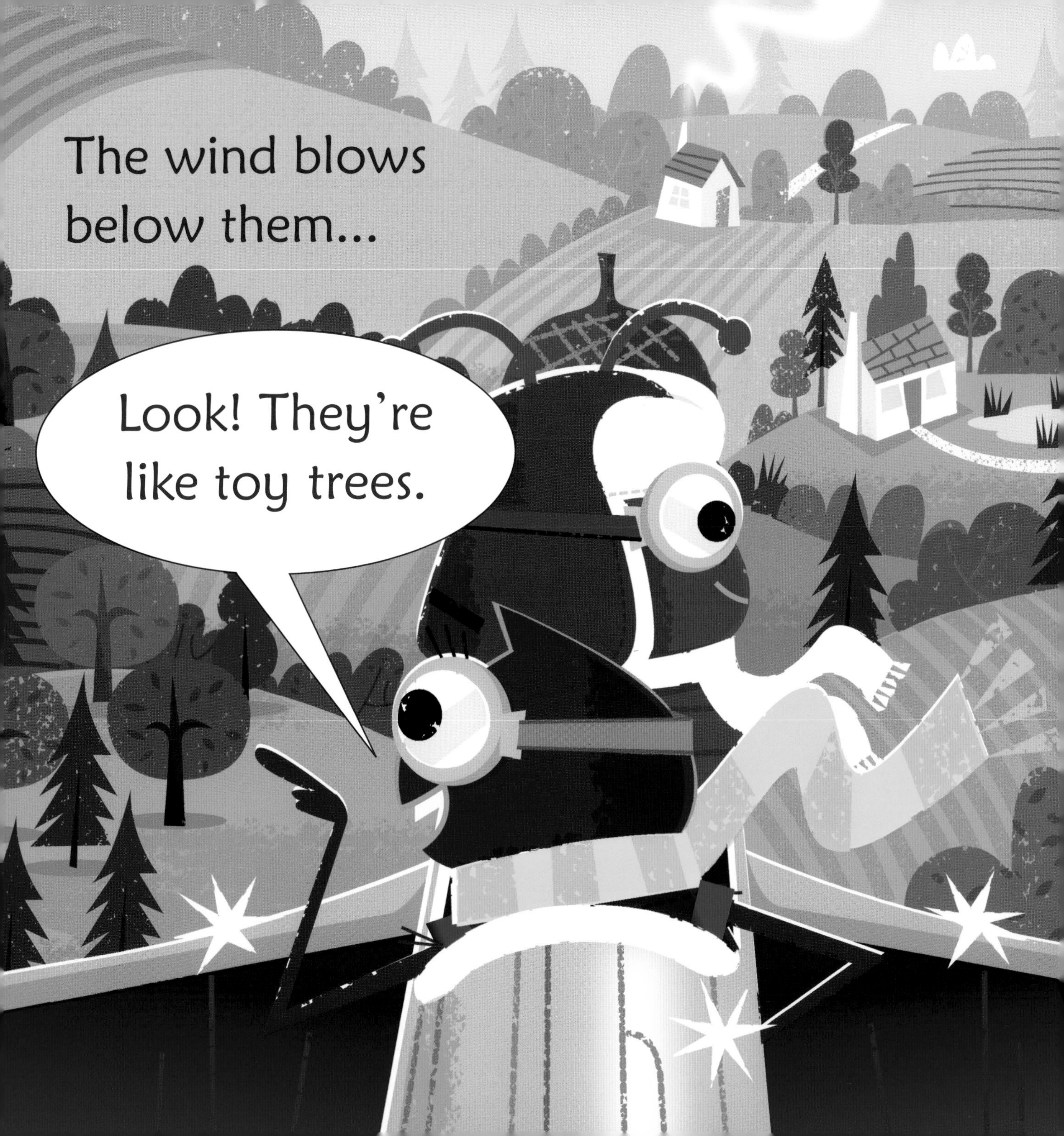

The wind starts to huff and to puff.
Thunder booms.

With a crack and a spark,
a bright lightning strike looms.

The glider is tossed up and down and around.

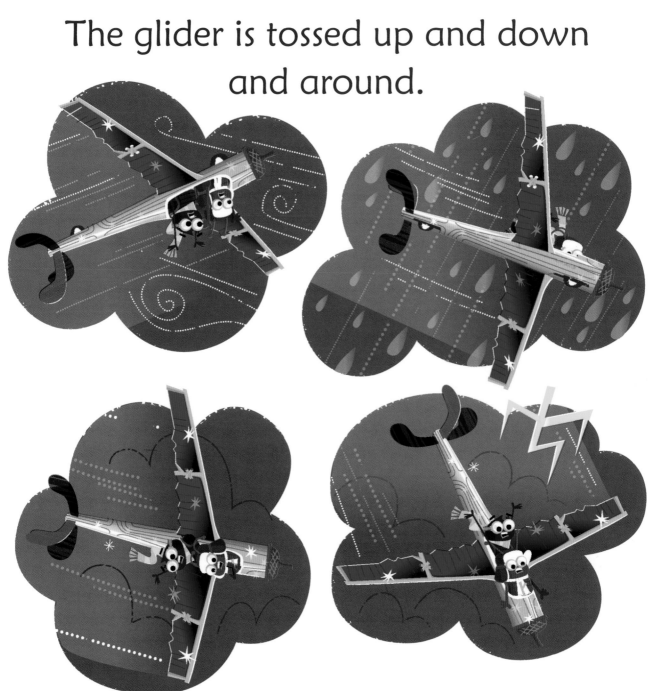

"All is lost!" Beetle splutters.
"We'll crash to the ground."

But Spider starts spinning.
Her legs are a blur.

"I'll save us!" she says,
with a *whizzz* and a *whirrr*.

They parachute down.

Now both have decided
life's best on the ground.

Hyena Ballerina

Ten students are wanted at Swan's Ballet School.

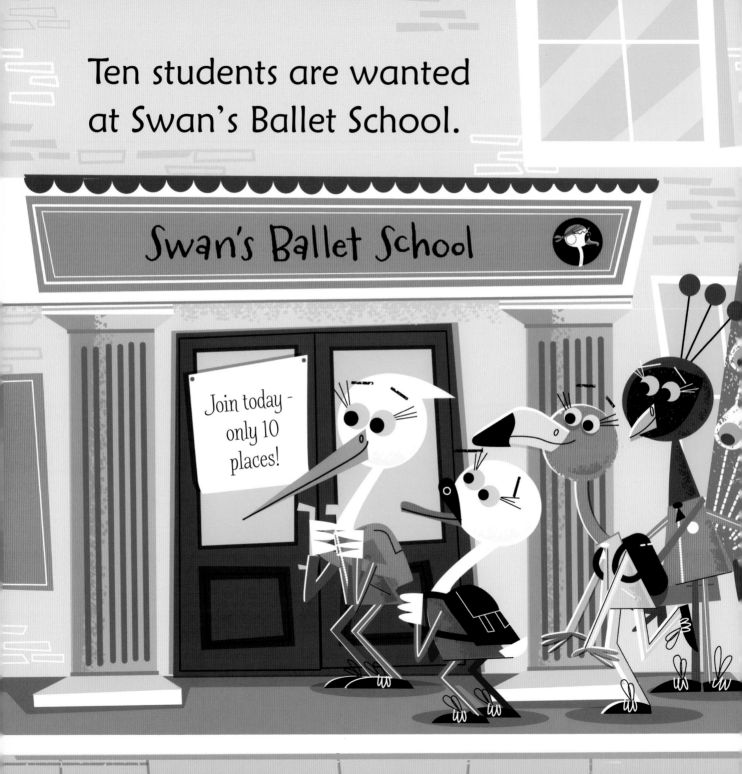

"What a chance!" cries Hyena.
"To dance will be cool."

"I think that I'm ready to prove
I can move...

...in my frilly silk tutu
and pink satin shoes."

Swan brings them together.

"Let's see what you've got."

Hyena springs forward
and spins on the spot.

She stands high
on tiptoe,

leans back
on a chair,

80

twirls lightly
in circles,

and floats
through the air.

"I can prance
like a princess...

...or glide
like a fairy."

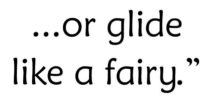

82

Swan soon loses interest.

"Too spotty
and hairy!"

Hyena feels weepy.

She sticks out her chin.

"What luck!" shouts out Duck.
"You're just what I need!

You must join my stage show. You're bound to succeed."

"My acts can jump hurdles,
or balance a ball,

STAGE DOOR

but ballet like that will
attract one and all."

"I'm spotted and furry.
You're sure you don't mind?"

STAGE DOOR

"Not a bit, don't you worry.
You'll fit in just fine."

As soon as they see her,
the crowds howl "Bravo!"

Hyena Ballerina is the star of the show.

Seal at the wheel

Seal gives a squeal.
She's seen a green sign.

For sale - one
speedboat

97

The speedboat is cheap.
She's aboard with a leap...

...honks the horn with her flipper. "Let's go!"

With a spin of the wheel
Seal speeds from the bay.

She goes faster and faster.

Hippo is wearing his new water skis.

Seal is scaring him.

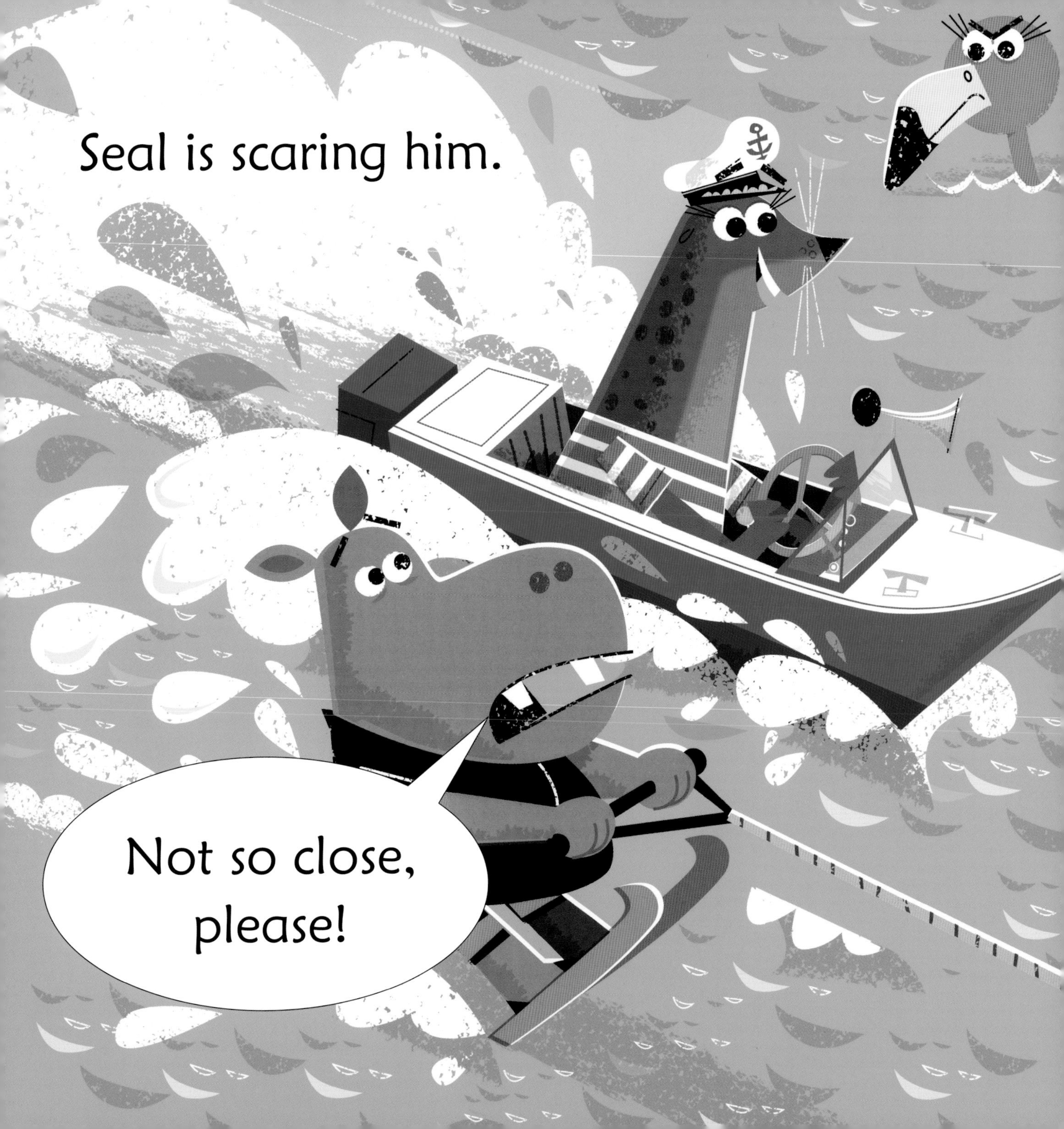

But Seal needs speed.
She is greedy for more.

She zips...

...Hippo flips

and he
surfs into
shore.

Seal's boat bounces wildly
and bumps over waves

as she weaves up and down.

Seal, will you behave!

"Enough is enough!"
Hippo roars from the bay.

"You make the sea rough. Seal, sail far away."

As Seal turns to leave...
a boat hits a rock.

Seal churns up the sea
as she speeds to the spot.

"Help! Our boat's leaking," some scared monkeys moan.

Seal hauls them to safety.

"I'll soon have you home."

Now Seal's still at the wheel,
speeding all round the bay.

She drives the town's lifeboat –
on call night and day.

Ape's great escape

Ape's in chains for stealing grapes.

Grape Thief
Gets Ten Years

631128

631128

But he has planned a great escape.

"The guards won't see me flee this jail.
My plan's so grand, it just can't fail."

"This key I made will set me free."

He bends the bars,

then jumps...

Whoopee!

His landing doesn't go to plan.
He falls slap, bang...into a can.

WET
PAINT

PAINT

PAINT

But Ape has made a great mistake...

The stones are really dozing crocs!

Ape screams and hollers.

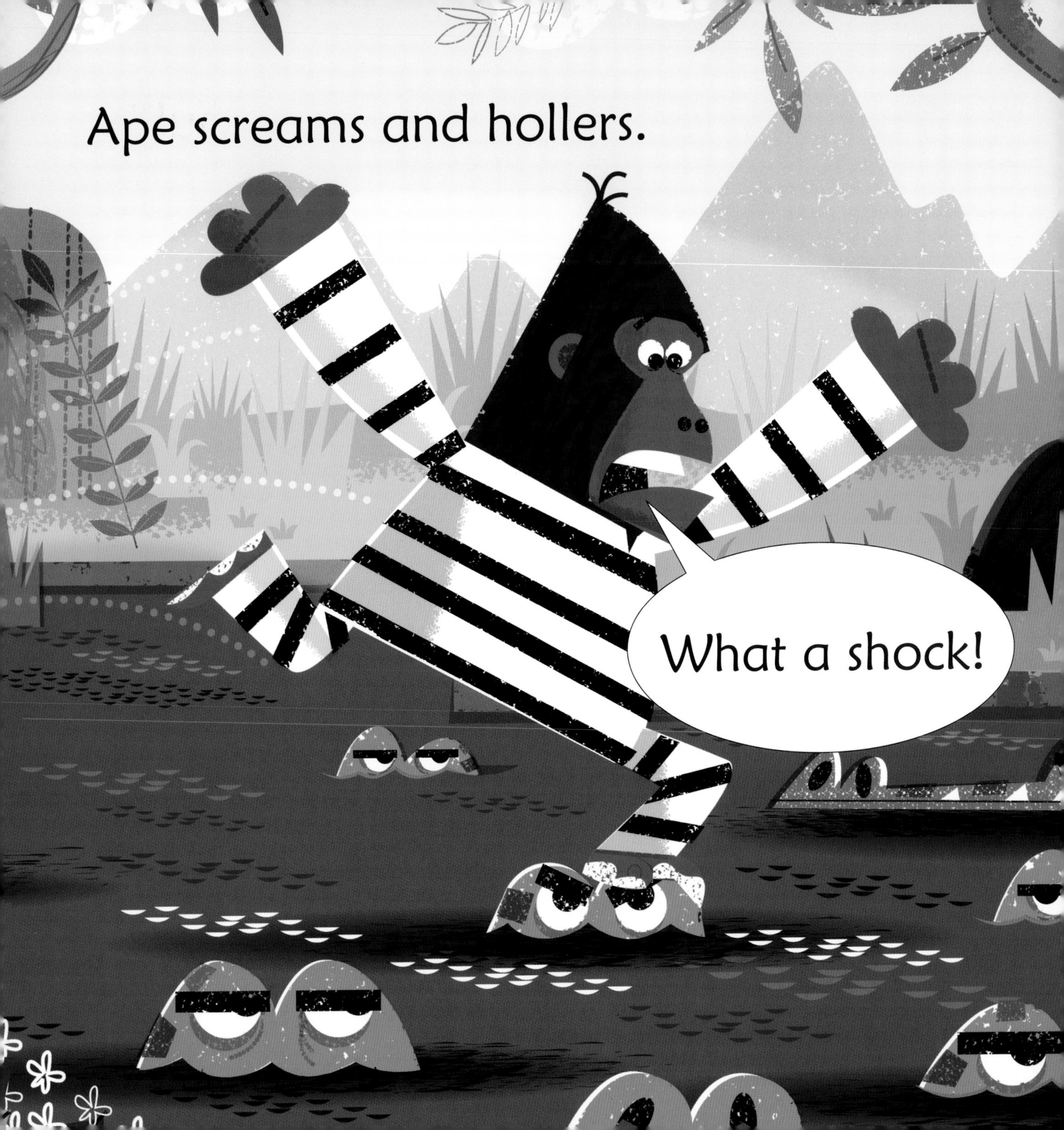

"I've reached the jungle. I'm okay!"

But a steamy swamp lies in the way.

"I'll swing across on this thick vine. One easy leap and I'll be fine."

Wrong once more, for it's a snake!

His hissing fit makes poor Ape quake.

Soon the mountains are in view.
"I'm nearly home," cheers Ape.

Woo-hoo!

But silly Ape's loud yell of hope...

brings boulders rolling down the slope.

At last Ape makes it to his cave.
"I'm home!" gasps Ape.

133

"Come out! Come out!"

Ape gives a frown.
The prison guards have
tracked him down!

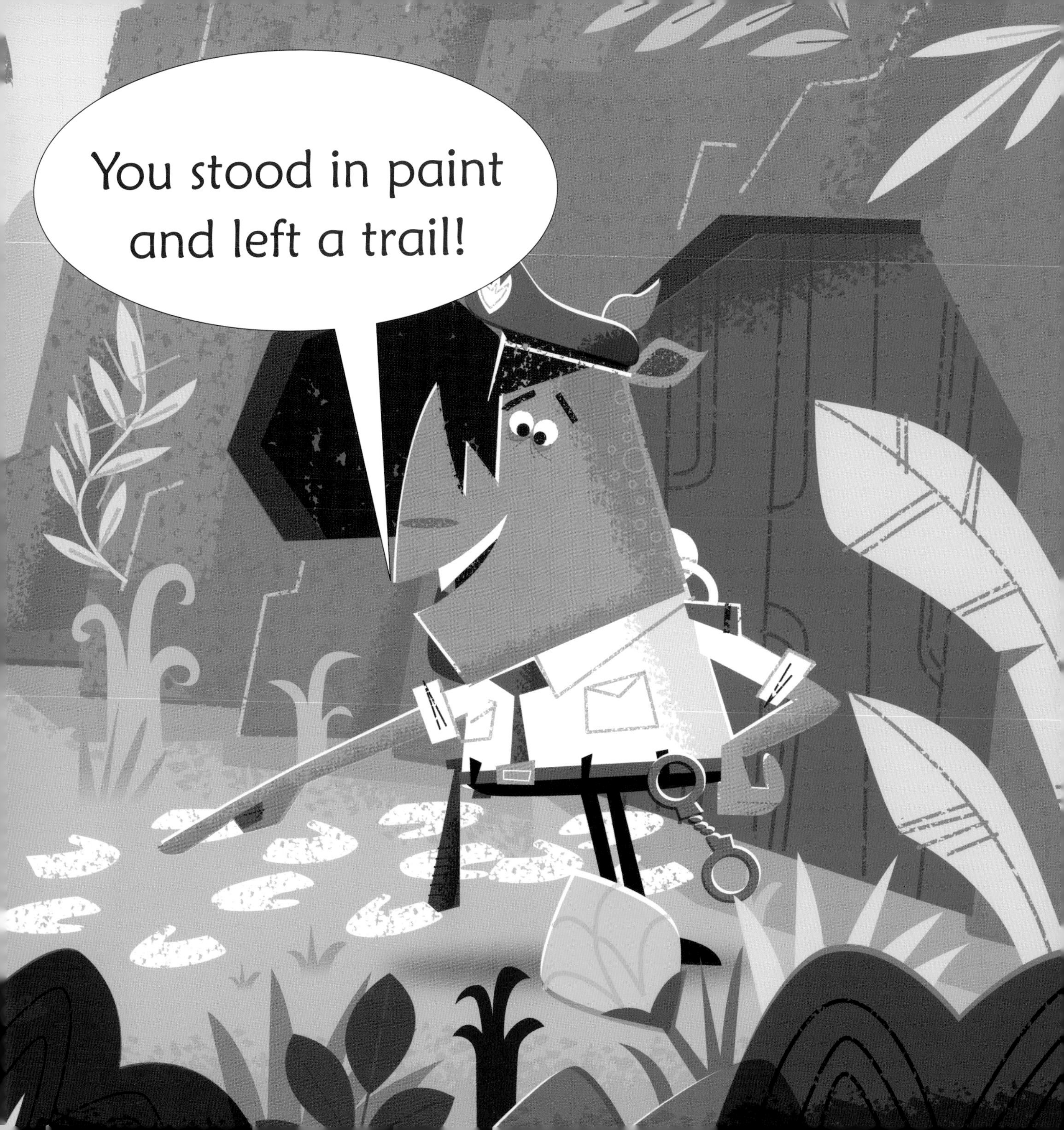
You stood in paint and left a trail!

Puzzles

Puzzle 1

Can you find the words that rhyme?

snake   day   prance
bay   slide   lake
chance   quake   glide
ride   dance   way

Puzzle 2

One word is wrong in this speech bubble.
What should it say?

We are crying!

Puzzle 3

Can you find these things in the picture?

Chimp   Cheetah   Frog

gate   crate

Puzzle 4

One word in each sentence is missing.
Can you say which word goes where?

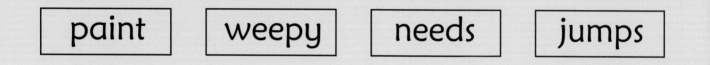

| paint | weepy | needs | jumps |

1. She ----- in the tub.

2. Hyena feels -----.

3. You stood in -----.

4. Seal ----- speed.

Puzzle 5

Choose the right speech bubble for each picture.

Answers to puzzles

Puzzle 1

snake   →   quake   →   lake

bay   →   day   →   way

chance   →   dance   →   prance

ride   →   slide   →   glide

Puzzle 2

Puzzle 3

crate

Cheetah

Frog

gate

Chimp